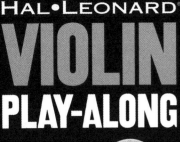

HAL•LEONARD®

VIOLIN PLAY-ALONG

AUDIO ACCESS INCLUDED

THE PIANO GUYS
Christmas Together

CONTENTS

PLAYBACK+
Speed • Pitch • Balance • Loop

To access audio visit:
www.halleonard.com/mylibrary

Enter Code
4405-9951-7361-8122

Audio Arrangements by The Piano Guys

ISBN 978-1-5400-2094-9

HAL•LEONARD®
7777 W. BLUEMOUND RD. P.O. BOX 13819 MILWAUKEE, WI 53213

Visit Hal Leonard Online at
www.halleonard.com

O Holy Night/Ave Maria

O HOLY NIGHT
Words by Placide Cappeau
Music by Adolphe Adam
Arranged by Jon Schmidt
and Steven Sharp Nelson

AVE MARIA
By Charles Gounod
and Johann Sebastian Bach
Arranged by Jon Schmidt
and Steven Sharp Nelson

As performed by The Piano Guys

Mary, Did You Know?/
Corelli Christmas Concerto

MARY, DID YOU KNOW?
Words and Music by Mark Lowry
and Buddy Greene
Arranged by Al van der Beek
and Steven Sharp Nelson

CORELLI CHRISTMAS CONCERTO
By Arcangelo Corelli
Arranged by Al van der Beek
and Steven Sharp Nelson

Ode to Joy to the World

ODE TO JOY
By Ludwig van Beethoven
Arranged by Jon Schmidt,
Steven Sharp Nelson and Al van der Beek

JOY TO THE WORLD
By George Frideric Handel
Arranged by Jon Schmidt,
Steven Sharp Nelson and Al van der Beek

As performed by The Piano Guys

What Child Is This

Traditional
Arranged by Al van der Beek, Jon Schmidt and Steven Sharp Nelson

As performed by The Piano Guys

O Little One Sweet

By Johann Sebastian Bach
Arranged by Al van der Beek, Jon Schmidt and Steven Sharp Nelson

Gloria/Hark! The Herald Angels Sing

GLORIA
Words and Music by Al van der Beek
and Steven Sharp Nelson

HARK! THE HERALD ANGELS SING
Words and Music by
Charles Wesley
Arranged by Al van der Beek
and Steven Sharp Nelson

rit.

The Little Drummer Boy/
Do You Hear What I Hear

THE LITTLE DRUMMER BOY
Words and Music by Harry Simeone,
Henry Onorati and Katherine Davis
Arranged by Al van der Beek
and Steven Sharp Nelson

DO YOU HEAR WHAT I HEAR
Words and Music by Noel Regney
and Gloria Shayne
Arranged by Al van der Beek
and Steven Sharp Nelson

Opt. 8va to end

As performed by The Piano Guys

Silent Night, Holy Night

By Franz Gruber
Arranged by Al van der Beek, Jon Schmidt and Steven Sharp Nelson

As performed by The Piano Guys

The Manger

By Al van der Beek, Jon Schmidt and Steven Sharp Nelson

As performed by The Piano Guys

The Sweetest Gift

Words and Music by Craig Aven